READING COMMUNITY LIBRARY

THE GIANT DEVIL-DINGO

WRITTEN AND ILLUSTRATED BY
DICK ROUGHSEY

MACMILLAN PUBLISHING CO., INC.
New York

Copyright © 1973 Dick Roughsey
All rights reserved. No part of this book may be reproduced or transmitted
in any form or by any means, electronic or mechanical, including photocopying,
recording or by any information storage and retrieval system, without
permission in writing from the Publisher.
Macmillan Publishing Co., Inc., 866 Third Avenue, New York, N.Y. 10022
First American edition, 1975
Printed in the United States of America

1 2 3 4 5 6 7 8 9 10

Library of Congress Cataloging in Publication Data

Roughsey, Dick.   The giant devil-dingo.
[1. Australian aborigines—Legends] I. Title.
PZ8.1.R754Gi3   299'.9   75-14210   ISBN 0-02-777840-1

THE GIANT DEVIL-DINGO

Away off in Dreamtime, old Eelgin the grasshopper woman and Gaiya the giant devil-dingo came travelling into Cape York. Gaiya was savage and huge, being much bigger than a horse. Old Eelgin was boss of that dingo and used him to hunt and kill men for food.

One day when Gaiya was away hunting, two young men came along to Eelgin's camp. They were the Chooku-chooku, or butcher-bird brothers. Old Eelgin saw them coming and called out, "You can camp here, boys." But the Chooku-chooku were afraid of Gaiya and did not trust Eelgin.

So they travelled on. As soon as they were out of sight down the sandy creek the butcher-bird brothers began to run away swiftly. Gaiya came back some time after the boys had gone, and Eelgin scolded him.

"Where have you been? You're too late now. There were two nice fat young men here, but they've gone. Come and I will put you on their tracks." And Eelgin set her devil-dingo on the tracks of the butcher-bird brothers.

The brothers knew that Gaiya would soon be after them and they travelled on and on, not stopping to rest, running as fast as they could.

When they heard the dreadful howling of the giant devil-dingo coming faintly on the wind they ran faster, heading toward the north-east.

That huge devil-dingo chased those boys for days and nights right across Cape York peninsula.

When Gaiya was hunting and got on the track of someone, his awful howling could be heard many miles away, and his galloping shook the ground and sounded like distant thunder.

Always they heard his howling coming down the wind; he was getting closer and closer. The howling dog came on, following their tracks.

Far behind Gaiya old Eelgin, the grasshopper woman, hobbled along on a stick sooling her dog onward, sooling him after the two brothers.

The Chooku-chooku brothers ran on until they were near Barrow Point, where they came to a big rocky pass through the hills. The young brother said, "I am tired and can run no further. What will we do now?"

The older brother said, "We will try and spear him. You climb up that side and I'll climb up this side. We'll hide and when he comes through we'll spear him."

They then climbed up the sides of the pass and hid among the rocks.
The butcher-bird boys listened to the dog coming.
He came closer and closer and the howling became louder and louder.

Soon the ground began to shake under the galloping of the huge dingo, and the noise of his galloping rumbled like thunder. The younger brother said "There he is! I'll spear him."

But the older brother said, "No, that's only his tongue. Wait."

Again the younger brother said, "There he is! Now I'll spear him."

But again his older brother said, "No, that's only his head. Wait and spear the dog behind."

The older brother hid patiently until the dog's shoulders appeared in the pass. Then he began spearing Gaiya.

He speared and speared him, and when he had finished the younger brother started spearing from the other side.

He kept spearing until Gaiya staggered away, dying from his many wounds.

The butcher-bird brothers climbed down and finished killing Gaiya.

They called to all the people to come and cut up and share the meat of the giant devil-dingo. The brothers cut off the tip of Gaiya's tail.

The spirit of Gaiya was in that tail and the older brother said to it, "Now go back and meet your boss."

The people were cutting up Gaiya, and they asked Woodbarl the white cloud, a medicine man, what parts he wanted. "I want the kidneys and head," Woodbarl said.

"You people have all the flesh, but give me the bones and some of the skin also." He gathered up all the bones and other parts and took them away to the top of a mountain.

Old Eelgin was still hobbling along after her dog. She saw Gaiya coming and called: "Ah, so my dog has come back. Did you catch those nice fat boys?"

But the spirit Gaiya was angry with Eelgin for having set him on the tracks of the butcher-bird boys who had killed him, so he bit her on the nose.

The butcher-bird brothers came and killed Eelgin. They said to her spirit, "Now you go down to Barrow Point and stay there; that will be your place."

Up in the mountains Woodbarl, the medicine man, took the bones, the kidneys and the head and made two small dingoes, one male and one female.

He covered them with skin and blew down the mouths of the dogs until they came to life.

Then Woodbarl said to the male dingo, "Come on, you howl now." The dingo howled. "All right, lift up your back leg now." The dingo lifted up its back leg.

"All right, you are a good one. From now on you are a dingo and you won't eat people. You will be a friend to man and help him hunt for food."

Today the dingo is a friend of man, Eelgin has her home in the rock in the salt-arm by Barrow Point, and the marks where Gaiya bit Eelgin can be seen on the noses of all grasshoppers.

Butcher-birds have long sharp beaks like spears, and Woodbarl has his spirit home on Woolcooldin Island, just off Barrow Point.

ABOUT THIS LEGEND

The legend of Gaiya the giant devil-dingo belongs to several tribes in the lower Cape York peninsula.

I heard it first from my old friend Jugumu of the Gugu-Yalanji people. He said that unlike all the other animals and birds, the dingo was not a man in the beginning, but had always been a dog. Archaeologists say that the dingo was probably brought to Australia as a domestic dog by raft travellers, who arrived in the northwest of Australia between 7,000 and 10,000 years ago, and spread out across the continent from there.

My people, the Lardil of Mornington Island, also say that the first dingoes came from the west, across Arnhem land.

The dingo was very important in hunting and I have seen many sacred paintings of dingoes in secret caves in Cape York. In one of the caves, the dingo can be seen to be tracking a kangaroo which had been wounded by a spear.

Wild dingoes never attack people, and live on wallabies, other small animals and birds. In Cape York they also keep down the numbers of wild pigs.

When travelling through the bush we sometimes find litters of dingo pups in short burrows in creek banks or hollow logs.

They make useful pets and are very loyal, a true friend of man.

DICK ROUGHSEY